Finalist for the 2022 National Book Aw...
the PEN/Voelcker Award for Poetry C...
the NAACP Image Award for Outstanding Literary Work–Poetry

Longlisted for the Griffin Poetry Prize

Further praise for *Best Barbarian*

"[A] substantial and prodigiously intertextual new collection. . . . [T]he names, quotes, and allusions [in these poems] do not function as an overlay, but as fundamental elements of the warp and weft of the net of Reeves's verse, and his own art is both adroit and capacious enough to probe or connect, to complicate or amplify all he catches there. . . . [A]mid the brutalities of abuse, death, and decay, these poems both apprehend and enact a sometimes terrifying beauty." —Heather Green, *Poetry Foundation*

"*Best Barbarian*, Roger Reeves's terrific second collection, eruditely sets out to unite the Western literary canon with its omissions and oppressions. . . . What I find most moving in this collection is the way fatherhood frames Reeves's sense of the future and his reworking of the past." —Sandra Simonds, *New York Times Book Review*

"The mesmerizing second collection from Reeves reflects intergenerational racial trauma and personal tragedy with a remarkable balance of acute feeling and lyrical precision. . . . With vivid images and haunting, evocative language, Reeves memorably places the reader in the space where life and death intersect." —*Publishers Weekly*, starred review

"Reeves's haunting second collection . . . crafts a sweeping and powerful poetic topography. . . . Rich and cohesive, with remarkable depth and lyrical command, this work offers manifold discoveries. A book that reveals more with each reading." —*Library Journal*, starred review

"*Best Barbarian* is a twenty-first-century masterpiece. Borrowing and turning on its head the Western canon's repeated warnings of civilization's fall, Roger Reeves counters that the apocalypse ran contiguously with the inception and height of Western civilization because the white man's rise was contingent upon the destruction of Black personhood. From that perspective, Reeves sees America as a necropolis through which he leads us—like Virgil—down into the underworld, where we meet the shades of Emmett Till, Oya, and Ezra Pound, among others. *Best Barbarian* is rich, intertextual, brilliant, and unforgettable."

—Cathy Park Hong

"From Grendel to Gilgamesh, *Best Barbarian* reviews and retells the most ancient of stories so that Roger Reeves can tell his own. The capaciousness of these elegiac poems, their Whitmanian need to hold and see it all, mirrors this speaker's need to be known fully as a Black father, a man in love, a surviving citizen, a son to his mother, and an investigator of his father's whereabouts even after death. This book is an education on this history of the soul."

—Jericho Brown

"Roger Reeves conjures the losses—no, the thefts—at the root of the American story. *Best Barbarian* is a revelation and a form of reparation."

—Tracy K. Smith

"*Best Barbarian* is a wide-ranging, capacious, and deeply felt meditation on ruptures, the violences enacted across time and space, where myth and history collide. Through dazzling riffs and leaps of imagination across linguistic registers, Roger Reeves offers an alchemy for repair. The sheer musicality of the language—the way resilience and love sing—makes a once-broken thing even more beautiful."

—Natasha Trethewey

"I cannot overstate the brilliance of Roger Reeves. A sentence inside a Reeves poem is a score of breath; a scripture with texture and subtext; a tightrope of expansive, existential syntax. *Best Barbarian* is a monumental and elegiac tour de force. Peerless and unprecedented, it is one of the best books I've read in years."

—Terrance Hayes

ALSO BY ROGER REEVES

King Me

BEST BARBARIAN

Poems

ROGER REEVES

W. W. NORTON & COMPANY
Celebrating a Century of Independent Publishing

For information about permission to reproduce selections from this book, write to Permissions,
W. W. Norton & Company, Inc., 500 Fifth Avenue, New York, NY 10110

For information about special discounts for bulk purchases, please contact
W. W. Norton Special Sales at specialsales@wwnorton.com or 800-233-4830

Manufacturing by Lakeside Book Company
Production manager: Beth Steidle

Library of Congress Cataloging-in-Publication Data

Names: Reeves, Roger, author.
Title: Best Barbarian : poems / Roger Reeves.
Description: First Edition. | New York, NY : W. W. Norton & Company, [2022]
Identifiers: LCCN 2021052466 | ISBN 9780393609332 (hardcover) | ISBN 9780393609349 (epub)
Subjects: LCGFT: Poetry.
Classification: LCC PS3618.E4456 B47 2022 | DDC 811/.6—dc23
LC record available at https://lccn.loc.gov/2021052466

ISBN 978-1-324-06445-9 pbk.

W. W. Norton & Company, Inc., 500 Fifth Avenue, New York, N.Y. 10110
www.wwnorton.com

W. W. Norton & Company Ltd., 15 Carlisle Street, London W1D 3BS

1 2 3 4 5 6 7 8 9 0

For Naima, for encouraging me to risk beauty

CONTENTS

BEST BARBARIAN

GRENDEL

All lions must lean into something other than a roar:
James Baldwin, for instance, singing *Precious Lord*,
His voice as weary as water broken over his scalp
In a storefront Sanctified Church's baptismal pool
All those years ago when he wanted to be
Somebody's child and on fire in that being. Lord,
I want to be somebody's child and chosen
Water spilling over their scalp, water
Taking the shape of their longing, a deer
Diving into evening traffic and the furrow drawn
In the air over the hood of the car—power
And wanting to be something alive and open.
Lord, I want to be alive and open,
A glimpse of power: the shuffle of a mother's hand
Over a sleeping child's forehead
As if clearing the city's rust from its face
Which we mostly are: a halo of rust,
A glimpse of power—James Baldwin leaning
Into the word *light*, his voice jostling that single grain
In his throat as if he might drop it or
Already has. I am calling to that grain
Of light, to that gap between his teeth
Where the many-of-us fatherless sleep
And bear and be whatever darkness or leaping
Thing we can be. In James Baldwin's mouth,
My difficult beauty, my weak and worn,
My future as any number of angels,
Which is not unlike the beast, Grendel,
Coming out of the wild heaven into the hills
And halls of the mead house at the harpist's call

With absolute prophecy in his breast
And a desire for mercy, for a friend, an end
To drifting in loneliness, and in that coming
Down out of the hills, out of the trees, for once,
Bringing humans the best vision of themselves,
Which, of course, must be slaughtered.

WITHOUT THE PELT OF A LION

Rage: Sing, Goddess, of the on-top-of-love
And the president's *chronic angers*, his mouth, a burning
Bird of prey, *a flood of flames*, and nowhere not touched;
Nowhere, the peace he makes of the world with war,
Luxury, club, spear; the bodies of refugees
Left in the desert *to rot as feasts* for the hawk
And the hooked-tooth of the wild boars running
From one empire to another, their hunger
The engine of their political will and bewilderment.
It is the wild that makes the rose
Redundant. Nettle, thorn, stone, beaver
Dead in the ravine, rise, and approach us
With the harmony of death, which is the direction
All wounds close. Between the on-top-of-love
And the green stem the body makes of itself on a bed after,
The head of the rose scattered between hill, dale,
Pillow, star, mouth, sing, Beyoncé, of the burning
Heaven, the hurricanes and the little graves
That rise after, and the big graves and the foxes
And the broken treaties with the bee, the deer,
The dense wood, the Kurds, the rebels, and even the storm,
Sing of men and women without the pelt of a lion
Draped over their necks, walking out of a flood
With their young, their old sitting upon their shoulders,
Their household gods and the bones of the dead
Clutched in their laps, the flood water in their laps,
The water siring what next to lose, siring the beginning
Of loss. Begin with—and where are my notes
Of the recent disasters—the ministers and priests in the statehouse,
Their hands stretched out toward the president

Blessing the minor miracles of greater destruction—
The banning of exiles and the hungry and anyone
Who has had to leave their living for dead,
Anyone who has to give their young to the swelling
Hurricane, the desert, the hawk, the dogs;
Who knew the human was a breed of grief?

CHILDREN LISTEN

It turns out however that I was deeply
Mistaken about the end of the world
   The body in flames will not be the body
In flames but just a house fire ignored
   The black sails of that solitary burning
Boat rubbing along the legs of lovers
   Flung into a Roman sky by a carousel
The lovers too sick in their love
   To notice a man drenched in fire on a porch
Or a child aflame mistaken for a dog
   Mistaken for a child running to tell of a bomb
That did not knock before it entered
   In Gaza with its glad tidings of abundant joy
In Kazimierz a god is weeping
   In a window one golden hand raised
Above his head as if he's slipped
   On the slick rag of the future our human
Kindnesses unremarkable as the flies
   Rubbing their legs together while standing
On a slice of cantaloupe Children
   You were never meant to be human
You must be the grass
   You must grow wildly over the graves

STANDING IN THE ATLANTIC

We were after death and before. Rising
Out of the drowned kingdom,
Some walked in the direction of Mali
Toward the blue chant coming from the cow
Skin and string stretched over the calabash's mouth,
A kora carrying Timbuktu's salt market—
Its holler and gold—over the executioners,
The sharks' desolate dorsal fins cutting
The horizon, the ocean into before
And after I could no longer touch
My mother's name, the night her fingers
Make when they touch my eyelids
Which is the origin of night—
A woman's hand to your face, a fire after,
Walking beneath it until a bird lifts dawn
Over an orchid's screaming white head and the stone-
Colored cat crouching in the grass waiting
To pounce on dawn's light emissary
Drowning, drowning in dawn.
Some of the drowned walked through
The emptying waves toward the indigo
Bushes burning on an unknown shore,
Their names called on brick plantations,
In rows of cotton, the thorn of which
Mixed them down to blood and land
And someone calling out to them for rest,
A night, a forest, a snake to ride
Out of the marsh buckling down into heat,
Leech, and the crooked day laboring
Their laboring bodies, its fingers jammed

Into their mouths, prying their lips apart
As if to see into that little bit of privacy,
The darkness, covering their runagate
Runagate hearts. The memory of wood,
Tunisia burned; this call put into the dead
For rest, a forest, a snake to ride.
Do you not hear our names being called,
Said a man who carried the splinters
Of wood from the ship's belly beneath his nails.
Do you not hear your name?

THE ALPHABET, FOR NAIMA

A is for *almost, arriving,* my father's death.
B is for *bear,* which he does and does not do.
C is for *care* and *critics* and leaving them to their caskets.
D is for *damn,* which your father does not give but must.
E, for *empire*—a thing to impale, kill, break
Breach. F is for *farther* along we'll understand why
Fire greets us at every door and we've lost our way
In the sky. Now where, where should we turn?
G is for *good, the shy speechless sound of fruit
Falling from its tree.* Me, you, there in the woods
Watching the pines shatter shadow in the light
Wind. H is for *horses* in the high cotton,
The crack in their hooves carrying your grandfather
And your grandfather's grandfather down the hill
Until two stomps on the barn floor orphans them
Again, dust, dust. I is for *in,* as in *in* the blood we bear
All sorts of madness but bear, bear we must.
J is for *jaundiced,* which you never were.
K is for *keep.* Keep your wilderness wild, your caves neat.
L is *lift* and *lymph,* the node they cut
From beneath your grandfather's arm.
M is for *misery* which turns and breaks in
Though I wish it would not. Leaf
Leaning on a pond. Blood on a sock.
N is for *nature* and *nearly* and how I've come
To love; nearly, nearly I come to you, my falcon
Hood pulled tight; my talons tucked; Lord,
Let me not touch. O is for *out* and the *owl*
You say sits on your nose. P is for *please*
As in "Please, son, don't visit me"

And yet I visited and did not please and he would not
Touch your leaf, afraid his rot *would*
Make the petals fall. A lovely love—
No, not at all. Q is for *quince*, its yellow-breasted
Bell knocking against my father's death-bed
Window, the light, the light too on his dying
Bed, what you opened your mouth to and tried
To swallow. R is for *road* where we lay,
Sometime, because we wish not to exist
And wish and wish and wish. And must.
S is for . . .

IN REHEARSAL FOR THE FUNERAL

And the dead, who do not reach out to touch
The lighted windows, touch us here—in the mouth.
Something in me wants to say it again:
Death, a forgotten destination not yet known.

What am I returning to momentarily—
The teeth of the sea, the teeth of . . .
You wouldn't understand that after death,
My father's death, my shoulders through the air,
My ears in the loud, precious winter light,
My mind gathered in the crisis of whispering
To itself, whispering, death, a forgotten
Destination not yet known—all my handling—
At the shoulder, at the ear, the mind—done
At the edge of teeth. My daughter, barely
One, lifted over the edge of my father's
Casket—at the edge of my father's teeth.
All handling after death is done at the edge
Of teeth—the locust undoing the earth
To yell from the trees, and the rain, the rain,
And the smoke, smoke—and has not charity
Or light willing to light the windows
Or my father in his death, begging,
A child begging, begging to be born.

This, the mystery the dead mumble over
And over to us in our sleep, in our lovemaking
In the hotel room beneath the lamplight:
This is not over—our death; make us, make us here.

SOVEREIGN SILENCE, OR THE CITY

After Vincent Valdez's painting The City I

Empathy will not end
Genocide. It won't
Even delay it. There:

The children running from napalm into the palm of our vision.

Above the city,
A Klan rally wounding
All the light and what you cannot see.

Here, you
Expect another
Disaster, quartered and cracked,

Yoked and yellowed
Flogged and rabid
Translated into a gash or coffin,

A prison notebook
Neutered of its nude
Rage, dick in its hand—uncensored

Memoir of the Beaver
Pursued by trappers
For the tincture in its testicles,

And in order to keep whole
Tears off his own testicles.
And runs. Even a rose needs an exit

Strategy without the paparazzi
Of having to explain
"I woke up like this,

"I woke up like this" or worse:
"I was bought like this,
"I was bought and sold like this."

Flawless. The dogs and daughters
Of disaster refuse to crinkle
Paper into tinkling roses

Or revise fire and the bodies
They lie beneath
To escape a fire into anything else

Other than suffering, not a ba-dee-ya
Nor an inshallah, not a mamase
Nor a mamakusa, not a shin-shallah

Damyatta nor a Holy Ghost gospel
Stomp; the nightingale above
The dead beaver in the bushes

Sings not of the hurricane
Beating the bamboo into noise
But of the death trapped inside its body

Which is louder than any beauty,
Which is all the beauty ever known
Before and after genocide.

Go out and retrieve
Your dying from this field
You've not come to—until now.

COCAINE AND GOLD

I never wanted to be this far
Into the business of heaven
                    Chasing my father hunting
His soul in the corn and confusion of this harvest

            My father who is hidden
In the last sheaf of heaven maybe
            Heaven itself
                    My father the corn-wolf

        Who we must kill but is already dead
                We will learn nothing
Here of sacrifice or the cocaine
                Of beauty my hands

            Chattering in eulogy
Which is a search for order
                    Which is nothing but
            The elimination of beauty by artifice

        By artifice we cauterize
My father's drifting life
            A minor cosmetic surgery
Like liposuction a funeral is

            An elimination of nature by artifice
By artifice do you repeat yourself
        Very well then I repeat
                Myself as heaven as a golden harvest

As a broken ocean of corn
The search for beauty is
The elimination of death
Which requires dying

Which is the business of farming
Which no one cares to do
Anymore in America
And like dying we'd rather rent it out

Freedom without freedom
To hold your dying father up
To a razor beneath a golden light
And cut him finally in and out of the world

RAT AMONG THE PINES

Terror, tonight

Is the moon
Slipping from a rat's gray grasp,

Finding its way back
Into the sky, which is America—

A white moon
Leaning on the night's neck

With its hands in its pocket,
Moon hung calm above

Catastrophe, the police
Breaking the neck of a man

Who had just brushed summer's
First bead of rain from his eye-

Lashes. Who—knocking a Newport
Against a wrist, watching smoke

Break its head against a brick
Wall—is preparing to die

Unaware they are preparing to die.
Heavy the moon, silly the tasking

Of a rat with delaying death.
Terror, tonight

Is the candor of the earth
Where someone is preparing to die

And the earth receives that dying
With its hands in its pockets.

And the moon that once burnt the silk
Hump of a rat, back in the sky.

And my daughter hiding in the rose
Bushes, asking who, who the sirens

Have come to kill. And someone calling
It beautiful—summer, moon—

And someone dying beneath that beauty,
Which is America.

AMERICAN LANDSCAPING, PHILADELPHIA TO MOUNT VERNON

Who would have thought—too much simultaneity:
The Swan Planters hovering above the wind-beaten
Statue of the Virgin Mary that casts her gaze down
On the Re-Painted Lawn Jockey, his brown face
Spreading out over his white cap, a small rebellion
Or, merely, an inarticulate hand overzealous
In restoring Race back to its place in God after
Winter makes heathen the heaven of horticulture.
This is America calling: the golden pollen of Spring
Blinging every available sedan, stone porch, puddle,
And satin blouse hanging from a smiling white line
Into yellow salvation, or forgetfulness, a black dog,
Antique in its hunger for my daughter's hand through a fence,
My daughter, in her machine and wonder, willing
To give. It is as if every moment is praying
For whatever is above it or just outside of its grasp: the dog
For a hand, the Lawn Jockey holding his absent lantern
Out in front of him for the Virgin whose eyes,
No longer there, Januaried away by the blizzards,
Salt, and wind, stutter with a brown streak
I won't call bird shit but rusted water
Dripping from the corrugated roof above.
Even the flies, in the earliest part of the sentence,
Twitch above the sidewalk as if being accused
Of neglect, infanticide, murder, ending the empire
In order to start another in their own image.
But, what is an empire fashioned in the image of flies?

Mistake: it's not a lantern the Jockey holds
Out in front of him, but a black hitching ring
For masters to tether the tamed because they lack
Mastering, though not the Jockey, who stands on the wind
And paving stones like Jocko Graves, the slave
Of General Washington, who froze to death
Enfolded in snow on the banks of the Delaware River,
His lantern out in front of him awaiting his master's return
As he had been ordered, and Washington, so moved
By Graves' frozen obedience, constructs a statue
Of dead Graves holding a lamp at his plantation
Home in Mount Vernon. Even in death, a slave must
Labor though I knew nothing of these clothes
When, on a Ferris Wheel, overlooking the muddy
Syringed and bottled banks of Philadelphia, I kissed a girl
Through the tin smog and chemical plant perfume
And carried that kiss through the year, touching newspaper,
Edges of blankets, the backs of hamburger buns
To my lips to remember the dimming summer
Sheepishly backing out of a door it hurriedly burst through.
Only in America will the sons and daughters of slaves
Kiss the sons and daughters of their masters
And remember it as an opportunity to be human.

INTO THE WEST

". . . It would seem clear that no one can call upon Thee
Without knowing Thee," though Augustine writes of God, here,
Notorious for his absence, he could also be speaking of desire,
Pleasure, the tick of snow against the dry leaves
Which sends my daughter spinning on her heel, the sound of it—
"that, Daddy, that"; sometimes the world, its loitering
Joy is just a *that*, an absence that calls, demonstrates its over-there-
Ness, its being but without a proper name so a silence
Sounded as when I enter the clearing I once begged for,
You, at an instant, absolute and looking back at me
As if witnessing a calendar or road you've already passed through
So my face now in whatever wolf, vulture, or golden horn
Of pleasure a *that*, a ticking of snow against the wet road,
Nameless, *Thee*, where you've been and left the-body-of-that-
Being so I, so I hurry and press into your leaving
Like a leaf scuttling after the dream of itself,
Into the sharp-wet of the snow against the skin, on into the West
Where desire—and sometimes pleasure—is a type of faith
What you call me to in this spilling, this motion of night:
Your hair loose in the water of your back.
Your spine has become the eye you wish for me to see
Through, but I must close my two good eyes, which is the beginning
Of any apocalypse or rapture: our daughter or the day,
Us touching the North and South of each other without compass
Or rose, this stumbling, a type of faith, too, a seeing
But without the dependence on sight or some heavenly ruin
As signal of an end. It was like the deer outside
Gathering at the window licking the cold glass to smoke.

THE BROKEN FIELDS MENDED

These are really the thoughts of all men in all ages and lands, they are
    not original with me,
If they are not yours as much as mine they are nothing, or next to nothing,
. . . .
This is the grass that grows wherever the land is and the water is,
This is the common air that bathes the globe.

—WALT WHITMAN, "SONG OF MYSELF"

                And for once white not as disaster

Crash, or brash binding rope to hold up, down, or from but merely to hold

The ambling mule deer which we follow, the common thought between us,

Not out of a killing hunger but out of hunger to be led by another

Animal, out into the drifts and gold of drifting, listening to the houses and rooms,
    and the smoke

Over the moon, which is the smoke over our mouths which we gladly take

As the voice of the deer, which is the voice of winter and the field for which we are,

For once, in, not as deathbed, cudgel, or cage but as

Field, and so land and so thought moving as a deer across the evenness of evening
    bowing to night

Which is how I've come to think of happiness, a bowing in a field, mouth to the field,

And everywhere that is not black, white, and everywhere an animal

Drifting away into the bare thicket such that it becomes the thicket

And the field permitting its end which we touch, though not an end-end because
we are

Still in the field unable to relinquish the snow, which is the voice of the land

Past the death of its dying, which is past animal. Us. Here. I am closing my eyes

Trying to hold the field in its body of snow, trying to hold winter up to your eyes

Before it withers and the deer returns over the shoulder of a hunter or the road;

Here, the field and you in it moving as cry, as *shall run*, as my hand pulling at the
stars,

And the stars obeying—the grass and the dark and the world not always ending

Though mostly it is,

                              And the smoke rising from the field is the angel we burn
    into the snow.

It is like the future and past of us meeting above and below us, our something in
the way

Of disappearing, our something in the snow; though the deer past, though the
angel burned, stay with me,

Stay with me here in this common thought, in this winter which will be rolled
into a canyon ditch

And all the winters to come will wither in their seed because we've not taken care
of the earth

And so no longer will we have the warmth of snow, or water. Or air. Or you. Or
you. Or you.

AFTER THE FUNERAL

A white cat has come to sit on the backside of slaughter,
      To sit on a white bull bearing a necklace of pomegranates.
The cat has come not as any witness to a crucifixion
      Or a coronation, not as angel or symbol of some comfort
Creature, some benign break in the dying,
      But as human wish, as distraction from suffering.

My human wish: to keep my father's schizophrenia
      In his casket, to keep *that* below the earth, one from another,
Now and forever. In season and out.
      From mountain to mountain. In the trees and after. Amen.
Everything has come back to prayer, sitting in that delay,
      'Harrowing the fixities,' my father in me, in my clock,
My hoof, my feather, in the sprawling
      Armature and stars of I am. Lord, am I worthy?

Have I devotion? What body built? Of flood, of cancer,
      Of winter, of woman—Lord,
I pray as I've been taught—to keep nothing
      From my tongue, its palm, its golden mind
So it bees and be's with whatever it be's—rose, rain—Lord,
      Even her, even her who rises from this bed,
The naked two-ness of her filling the room such that she becomes the room—
      Lord, am I ready?

How shall I bear the coming madness if it is come?
      What disaster will I deliver to my daughter?
My human wish: distraction: a white cat,
      Balanced on the backside of a bull, slaughter

Far off, this delay, Lord, this delay I offer
  Because I own neither houses nor land, have not a hundred heads
Of cattle or of State grazing on grain in a golden-green field.
  Keep this coming distant, this sickness underground,

And if Lord I am, if I am to bear madness,
  Become the father who scratches the raw earth
With his hoof and snout, plowing the field
  As ox or ass because the mind says, *go, go*
Into the pasture not as ox or as ass but go, Ox,
  Go, Ass, then Lord, let me into the field, but make,
Lord, Diviner of the snowflake and master of fragments,
  A light, a golden light in a tree,

And there, have my daughter stare at its working
  The darkness in the green, in the leaves and red blooms,
While I, behind her, lick the tines of a fence
  And leap in the dust in front of a white cat
That has become my master, that I follow
  Out to a white bull bearing a necklace of pomegranates.

ECHO: FROM THE MOUNTAINS

Unicorns brought the news of human reason to the border
So we gassed them. It was unlike the echo of guitars in a stone
Cathedral or midnight's crow landing snow in a field of wheat.
Their deaths had a magpie's clarity for prophecy in the bits
Of mane, snagged flags in the tines of the border fence, prophecy
In the blood blotting the stones that winked at us as if saying *you too,*
You too will become the clock of your disappearance. Leviathan,
Nightstick, tear gas—the century, barely beyond its birth-
Rattle, had become a banker riding the greenback of a brown
Stallion to dust and bone. Who will shoot the century in the heart?
Who will take a selfie with the corpse wearing a sign that reads:
Your selfie will not save you from your corpse—the clock of it,
Its ruptured spleen, its begging and blank labor? Every century
Falls below the imagination of itself then takes the shape of its falling:
401K. Roth IRA. Short-term Bond Funds. Forest fire. Instagram.
A crow is the emperor of any domain that capitulates to the whistle
And weather of crows. No angel will come and bear these migrant
Deaths beyond this bird and human reason.
Someone called it a miracle—the gassing. That it could be done
Remotely. With various devices. And no one harmed.
My father, who is dead, said it reminded him of getting a haircut
On Good Friday: "One man closes his eyes, another cuts it off."
The mark of invisibility is often mistaken for the mark of absence;
All desire is shaped by the delusion of consent.
Who has not been an entryway shuddering in the wind
Of another's want, a rose nailed to some dark longing and bled?

SO, ECSTASY

And after LOVE had wept and eaten
The burning heart, my burning
Heart, and LOVE our Lord, Lord, Lord
So awakened but not in horror but, yes, berserk, so:

Human, so wanted beyond, so: ECSTASY,
So: not human but ALL as in without ORDER,
So wept, *made into the vessel that which must be made*,
Confronted: so less life and more,

So ECSTASY, finally legible, without the formal
DRAG of the body, leaf upon leaf in the morning
Street, so past desire as a tree just beyond a wooden fence,

Invisible, in its possession and slow convulsions,
Hemorrhaging between night and the memory
Of waking as the wind, the night, the bleeding stars
Which is how I awaken in you, as you. Inside. Out. Begun.

. . .

Which has no memory, ECSTASY, beginning
In the middle, always late but slightly on time,
The way I touch you, which is an asking,
Berserk as any nag beauty so LOVE

Without the chaste harnesses of redemption, Us:
Somewhere after, tossed, like money fleeced of its money,
Grip, so wild and without use, so useful because without
Expectation, so without error, so desire moving backward,

Beyond opinion or the pinions of the body—so ECSTASY,
My mouth staggering to close upon your nipple—
Tree dwindling down to its birth-seed, PROGRESS:

Finally, a music made without progress or the hint
Of ascension, which is how ascension is reached
Rain banally falling into a field
Unaware a whole forest of elms rising from it in three days.

AFTER DEATH

To get the light and dead coming through
The window without distinguishing one
From the other is the day with and without
Its mastery, stumbling upon a dead deer
In a neighbor's field, knowing it was left
There for you not as muse but as memory
Dropped, broken off. Death no longer concerned
With this beast that once covered a field
With the white breath of its longing
Because the animal is beyond Death,
And *Death has no interest* in what is beyond
It, so now it's off to stare at the barely-
Standing-there Drunk swaying beneath two scythes
Hanging on two boards above his raised eyes,
The afternoon drifting into doorways,
Death now in a pocket of pines, in the thick
Hair of a boy who turns a skunk over
With a stick, watching the Christmas of its intestines
Steam in the snow. Death touching the boy
Where it is he will know him—beneath the arm
As if raising him up to this common
Understanding. Desire is everywhere
In this field, even in me who is not
In this field but, from my many windows,
Watching the night's dark light fall and dwell
In its falling which sends me stumbling
To my newborn's invisible breathing,
Wanting to ensure the invisible

Holds, my fig-branch finger stretched beneath her
Nose, me wondering: what is beyond death?
And what is this rage in darkness?
And my father, what is he other than dead,
Rage and so much light and so much light?

CYCLOPS AND BALTHAZAR

I was not a very good dog in my former life. I bit
My owner, James, often. When he prayed, I howled
His one eye opening. He said I sounded like a cyclops
That had fallen into a ravine. I heard raven. As I said,
I was not a very good dog, more so a ravine
Bringing the howling darkness to my owner's ears.
A raven that took flight only when watching the other ravens
Lift from the pines like scabs ripped open to reveal
What life runneth under. Toward the end of my life,
A donkey with a white flower and a crown of leaves
Befriended me at the edge of a field. At night,
His head moved "like a veil across the stars"
Revealing for me, for the first time, the stars.
Balthazar, the donkey, once asked me if I ever thought
Of the consciousness of trees, their reflection
In the river. Or if there was an etiquette to dying.
I said, "Stop that. You sound like a man
With his back to heaven." He said, "Someone will
Always have their back to heaven," then walked
Into a pasture of sheep and died. "Goliath,
Goliath," said the sheep's bells around their necks.
"No," I said. "Balthazar. It is Balthazar that has died."
And when I called out to him behind the door of the house
Of the dead, the night called back in my own voice.
And I, like a good dog, ran toward it with both eyes closed.

MOTHER'S DAY

The coyote runs to you as if you were the invisible rabbit
Suddenly sprung from the bush and meant to be eaten;

Then, as if the crow that leapt from the stone ledge
Shook the sky and restored the coyote his right vision,

The brush wolf veered back into the pines, its body
Taking the brown shape of the afternoon's swaying

Ache expressed in the branches. More than transfigurations,
There are so many moments of grace I will never understand—

Mint growing at the entrance of a graveyard, 'the wind
Resting its cheek on the ground,' the sun slipping

Into a boy's pocket and warming an unpeeled orange,
Stars echoing in the leaves of the live oak,

Basil on sliced tomatoes, the fish below the ice, roses
Rising through the red, green, then golden harvest

In the worst autumn, winter, spring, your foot,
Your foot across mine in bed on a day the dead walked

Into our house without taking off their shoes;
Without mint on their tongues, the dead came,

My father, your brother, through a hole in the floor.
They showed us where 'the vermin eat their bodies

As if they were old clothes, filthy, discarded.'
They showed us their old clothes

Until the night took on the hue of bone. They
Entered and entered us as if interring snow.

And, we went to bed underneath the hue of bone,
A house of snow, but then your foot, your foot

Across mine in bed, the perfect weight of it,
As if it were a gate closing,

A bowl restored backwards from its shattering
So its shattering still somewhere inside it and water,

Water, too—your foot, your foot across mine,
Stars echoing in the leaves of the live oak,

In the dead, the coyote wearing the invisible shape
Of the afternoon and running toward us again.

SECOND PLAGUE YEAR, BLACK SPOTS ON THE ROSE

The children ask of the opposite of deer—
Of casual terror—why
Must the dead wear white bags

Around their dying. I don't want to forget
This. Black spots on the rose,
The deer eating the black spots and the rose.

The tick-tock of crows smudging the evening
Sky, moving their ink across our faces
Until night, in its earthly reticence, comes

And the little fires left in us,
The little fires not put out by disease or worry,
The little fires, heavy

As a rusted-out refrigerator and on our backs, up a hill—
We lift and dance,
Lift and dance to the little fires, to the windows,

To whatever sound
We can drive out of them
Or the little boxes of electricity and desire we pray to.

I don't want to forget this: the dead
In the mouths of the children,
Gauze packed into their bloody gums,

My child pointing at the deer laying in the yard,
A white sack of mucus and steam
Falling from her

And when the little noun refused
Its mother's licking and would not rise to meet her,
The mother licking anyway.

POEM, IN AN OLD LANGUAGE

Many are the names of the Gods,
And many, the Gods with no names.

Many are the shadows cast by wasp,
Plow, and many born of shadows,

Of wasp dying in the flesh of the fig,
Of plow figging the flesh of the land.

Many have come back to the land,
The house of their former occupation,

Found their beds slept in, their flour
Sifted, baked into small loaves of bread

Cooling on a white windowsill
That once held salt and several mistakes,

Of which a rose was one. Its scent still
By the door. The rose, in its "tongue of flame,"

"Crowned knot of fire," is an old language
Which the New Masters believe better

Burned, buried, brightened
By a cemetery wall. The corpse of which—

Spine of the rose less its thorn and flame—
They are. Foolish, the New Masters;

What they called a beginning was their end,
Which began when they called themselves

Master—their beginning, their end
Was not the wasp rising again

In the flesh of the fig but the whole grove
Burned so an absent God might speak.

And we might listen.

. . .

Listen:

Infinite the Gods who are born of the dead.
Infinite the men who find them in trees burning,

Taking them down into the city,
Into the roads, into the war and warehouses

So that we might worship, might
Give birth to our deaths. Listen:

. . .

Infinite the burning, the ordinary atrocities
The mountains slopped to rag, the boast of black smoke

In which people burn.

Listen:

. . .

Infinite the forms of men breaking
The air with *incandescent terror.*

Infinite the cemetery walls, us coming in
Under their shadow, the wave of which we are.

THE END OF GHASSAN KANAFANI

Is this not a conversation between the sword and the neck—
This bone-flower elegy, this man who found his work
On the road and lay down with it, dead, on the road, this peace
Which is not peace but the neck after the sword, the bomb after
Blowing out all the windows of Ghassan Kanafani's house, this blood
In the driveway, his niece dead too, and his son, his son
Banging his head against the house wall, the bone of his father,
The ash gathering in his hair; is grief not a conversation
Between a house and a head; this liberation still on the road, this man
Who Sorrow speaks of willingly, who leaves his coffin
On the road below the smoke over the sick moon.
We have finally arrived at the end of the poem,
The moon sick, Kanafani standing at its edge,
Asking me: *What are you loyal to other than death?*

. . .

Envoi

What are you loyal to other than death?
To you, the dead, and what is not dead in your death.

. . .

And, what is not dead in your death? The children
At the gates of the city asking us to break the city,

. . .

To let the leopard in and the horse and the oak

54

And the grain of wheat to tear the sky with its abundance,

. . .

And when the bomb hidden in the basement of a church
Explodes, to weep and gnash and let and let

. . .

The four dead girls who've been driven in and out of the poem
By history and a bomb in the basement of a church

. . .

To haunt the plate of the nation, to travel in the husk
And ears of corn going to market, to sit on the Senators' plates,

. . .

To hear in the corn taloned at the end of their forks, the girls
To feel in the kernels digging into their gums, the girls,

. . .

To know the food in their mouths is the death of things—
Life, it is at every window. It's what rots the Senators' teeth.

DOMESTIC VIOLENCE

Let us descend into the blind world now
                    —*INFERNO*, CANTO IV, *DIVINE COMEDY*

As above, so below; as below, so above.
                              —*THE KYBALION*

A Lowcountry marsh trembles with the blood of an African
Who refused to climb out of the salt and mud of the bay
And quite literally lost his head. A hunter named Hunter
Waits for the man's wounds to close and for him to rise
Again. Some call this festive cruelty Paradise. Pleasure.
Demby, the African made to rise and suffer another shot,
Calls it the Afterlife, the unceasing blind world of death
He welcomed expecting the end to his captivity and exile.
But there is no end to the perfecting of cruelty even now
In the Afterlife, where a hawk humped up in the high weeds
And a house on fire are a congruent sadness, a brief history
Of nature's one duty for flesh—*decay, decay, decay* . . .
Sometimes, it is as if every bird in the Afterlife trills this
One song. And I forget who I am, but then I look down
At my feet shuffling in darkness and hear my name—
Till . . . Till . . . Till . . . And I know I am no farmer, blade
Or mule driven over some roach-ragged road to field
And fray, and sometimes I forget how I came here to After-
Life, to pleasure, to this domestic violence, to drive and be
Driven, and then I look down at my hands. It is a war
That brought you this peace, a war that brought you this peace.

Then, I heard a question: shall we kill all of the masters?
And before I brokered an answer, I heard a voice say:
"Then, we must kill ourselves, first. And who will
Be left to kill the masters?" I turned to find nothing
But a boy in a tree and a girl beside him, their heads
Tolling in the wind like pecker-fretted fruit. Voice, I said,
Come now or do not come at all. And there, a man
I had seen before scratching in dust next to a drill field
With a dictionary and a strange astronomy for a face.
Ezra, is that you, I asked. "The peasants' bent shoulders,
Odysseus and the dead bullock—call me whatever you'd like.
I come to every name like a white ox toward Pisa
And the butcher's road. I come to Paradise dragged
By the hair . . . with one day's reading and surrendered
Temple." You do talk funny, I said. "He do the police
In different voices," he said. And when all the voices
sound like the police, I said, kill all the voices. And so ran.
I ran from Ezra who ran after me and demanded he be
My guide. "There is no running from the forest of men.
There is no running from men." I'll be damned, I said—
But before I could finish Ezra said, "That's right. Be damned.

Be here taloned and tumbling the sky down in Paradise.
Here. Be in your cage and free." But here is not the here
I seek nor sought. For that here harangues me
And I might as well be the nigger coming over
The obstacle fence, a periplum of certain disaster,
A choir of empty cups sitting loudly before the famished,
Your prince, dear Ezra, hanging by his heels in the piazza,
The sprezzatura of maggots rummaging the round heart
For its divinity and pulse. Ezra, nothing of you but the dead.
And so, I ran past the possum running through the skull
Holes of a dead man lying in the fog that licked them

Into a wet testimony, the possum testifying, too, to their death—
Coming, going, in ruins and floating out, out, beyond
Their murders and dropped plates, out beyond the Thames-ish
Rivers and their drowning traditions. And then I looked back
And saw Ezra. He had come to his cage and could go no farther.
"Till," he said. "Bring me up from beneath these decks,
One slaver to another." He winked and I winked back,
Handed him the katydid buzzing in my pocket, as I had done
Before, dug a trench around him as another had done before,
Then said, "Ezra, be here in your cage and free," and ran.

And then I came upon a mountain and then a chasm
For which there was no bridge and so turned back
To find a possum running behind me, and I asked him,
Dear Possum, what do we do with this darkness
Between us, and the possum said nothing and ran on
Into the darkness, into the chasm and fell speaking of
The end of touch, the desire to forget desire, shadows,
The fear in a handful of dust, a woman's mouth,
Fear I had known of and visited though now I cringed
At the thought of that violence, the violence that I brought—
And so thought to throw myself into that chasm
When a hand touched my shoulder, a voice said, "Not now,
Maybe never. On we go, dear boy, through this weather.
Let's find us another theory of light. Or darkness."
Then, she laughed, for it was a woman with a lit darkness
And a careful chin, glasses, her body a tin of tender.
What do you know of me, I asked. She said, "Louis,
I know of you as I know fog—that it comes on
Through the alleys and past the dead boys and girls
Who had not wanted to die in those alleys and ornament
The city's sight. Louis," she said. "I've known all your light.

But do you know mine?" And I hadn't, I hadn't.
"I was a taken city burning," she said, "a burning house
Built to heal the sick, a sick house full of healing,
The owl, moccasin, and panther—a rising
For which there has never been such risen, the total
Black. I is the total black. Flame and fox and knot
Of the what-nots you would have forgotten if not for me,
I am perfect fucking memory, no-dominion-defied,
The god-head-glitter-gussied-up-for-the-going-down."
And though I thought I saw I had not seen. Instead
Of one body, three. Women. And who and who and who,
I asked. They laughed at my asking and said, "You
Wouldn't know us, but we will tell you our names—
Mother, Song, and Holy Yoke. Audre, Gwendolyn,
And Lucille. Follow us. Or heel." And where
And where should I follow you? They did not answer,
Instead, they walked on the edge of the abyss
Laughing as if the abyss. "We are what is the what-not,
The ever shimmying out of the never-wound.
Louis, do you follow or do you fall,"
They said. "Are you short or is you tall?"

And on and on they played, pleasured, and pigeoned
With each other, kiting sound and word between them
As I have seen lovers do, passing cigarettes and smoke
From one mouth to another, the smoke the shared body
Of a God that has no master or mastering plan
Other than abiding in darkness, abiding in both
Its coronation and crucifixion. On and on we walked.
And I followed. Beyond the bears chortling pears
From Augustine's outstretched hand, out beyond the river
Scissoring the changing maple, its leaves ambering
Then auburn then green each time a child appeared

And touched its trunk. We stopped, watched. I asked
Who are they. And the one full of light and knives answered,
Waving at a few who journeyed to the edge of the water
But did not wade in. And why don't they wade in,
I asked. She snickered, quieted, then said, "Wind
And foxes, what was never mine but was and was."
As if she knew I did not understand, continued, "The ones
I got but did not get, the wild hair they could not grow
But scratches me now as it did once in a dream.
Our abortions, Louis, our ones given and gave. D'em.

The ones given all of their years at once. And none
Or never." And when she spoke, I saw another come
To the shore and wave at me, a boy given and gave, the crushed-
Color of late evening long after the pickers have come
In and settled near a pot of ox bones boiling in the evening
Of their own water, once again predicting the arch
And strange astronomy of the flesh and its march march
March to October and the battered soil. I mean I turned
From the one waving because I could not be beneath
The stairs of his steering and stare. Paradise,
Why do you bring me to such weather? Why
Would any man come down from his noose for this?
"Because coming down is exactly the point.
All heavens lesser and below heaven. Noose, not . . .
You came to see what has become of death . . ."
The women spoke as one who had many tongues:
All Holy Ghost and gut of a river gabbling over the white
Stones. And where are we going, I asked.
"Where language begins, Till.
                    Paradise. But over there."

                ·   ·   ·

And wasn't this paradise that I had entered

Through the thick marsh waters out of the cane

The crowds fleeced of their living flesh at the far bank

The intubated children with their gas mask

Hanging from their hands and wandering

The sand in wet hospital gowns in this their new cancer

Wasn't this paradise

A boy headphoned and heart drunk

Swaying at the back off the crowd mumbling to himself

We started at the bottom now we're here

We started at the bottom now the whole crew is fucking here

Wasn't this paradise

The pigeons and finches flying back out

Of the pane-glassed windows they crashed through

The glass behind them opening and closing

Like some never and wound

Diastole systole the valve collapsing

In its own beating sickness   wasn't this paradise

The rows and rows of men on horse back

The gnashing of hoof in the heather

Everything ready to gallop or be galloped

Except the men and women herded

Into some queer parliament   wasn't this paradise

To refuse to run at the behest of some horsemen

The running   how they got here   wasn't this

Paradise the end of running

"Wasn't this paradise," asked a man
Named Priam, a fence post cutting his head
Into two hemispheres, his mutilations and wounds
Closing, his two torn ears fluttering
Upward from a sack hanging from a horseman's white

Mare. "I was born with water in my voice,
The problem of a fouled well, the lord
Gives us many, and I am the many given
But he, even as he gives, does not give a given to take
Or a given permitted to take. You see,"
And Priam stretched his hand over the people,
"We were a given taken and taken as a given.
I mean we are a transgressed light, a transgressed
People. We've been given this death. And now
You want us to take another death, but a man
Or woman can only take their one death.
And we have taken, we have taken, we have
Taken." With each "taken" he pointed to the many,
To the boy with headphones who could be heard
Singing "we started from the bottom, now here,"
To Demby to Aunt Hester to Sandra Bland,

To Freddie Gray to Walter Scott to Eric Garner,
His throat still crushed in his one hand
Though in his other, a clutch of dry seeds
And wherever he stepped a patch of trees sprouted.
"Guides," I asked, "where have I entered?" The names
Of the dead rolled out along the field; the whole
Field was counted—every maple, mango, muscadine
Larkspur, ant, vine, and moss—and there was no
Answer from my guides. They stood beyond
The queer parliament of the dead, and so I rushed over
But could not make it to their portion of the field,
The edge disappearing, the banks moving back from me.
"We are not permitted," they said. "We are not
The dead of this dead. A different light. But go."
And then I heard my name; well, not my name
But the name of my name, "Till, Till, Till."

And the men on the horses brought a boy up,
His hands tied, and one spoke, "It is a god
Who has given us this rest, this after and land,
This mount and tarry for the good works
Of our living. Why should we reject our peace?

No harm lasts; we live forever in our wounds."
The man pulled his burgundy riding coat
To the side and blood ran waterfall from his ribs,
Onto his white britches. "And maybe," a woman
Spoke, "your wounds would close if you would let ours."
"But I am content in my wounds," he said
And closed his riding robe though the blood labored
And labored. "I am content in my wounds.
Maybe we've been given to you to teach
You how to be content in yours," he said.
"Such is given, such is given of God,
of a God." The rider laughed and threw his head
Backward and there a wound, too, where his neck
Coupled with the skull, and the wound spoke
But not the speech of the mouth but the speech of reason
But not the reason of Plato, Virgil, Foucault
Or the stars maddening the night with their bursts
Of madness, their dying in the night's hair,
But the reason of the spear that pierces
The skull and slides through the chin, letting
The darkness down, letting all the darkness down.

"I see no God here nor one to come. Let down,
Let down from your mount and execution
Garden. You are no Nebuchadnezzar.
But if you keep up this reckless lord
And master, I will show you what beast

You are from the inside out, give the leaves
And spears of grass below a winter washing
In your love." The men on mounts shook
Their reins and laughed. "And who are you,"
They asked. "The perfection of water,"
She answered. "The perfection of water."
The mounted man with blood running from his skull,
Shook the rope holding the neck of the boy, Till.
"Well," he said, "call me the perfection
Of slaughter. Teacher. Farmer. Daughter, move,
I will till this after and life and land
With whatever blade I choose, given or not.
Have you misunderstood dominion—or me?"
"I have and I have not," she said. "I am
Not your daughter. I am Oya-Oya
The mother of your slaughter. The mother

Of this order." The woman, Oya, bent down, touched
The dry clods of soil. "Here, here is your god."
She held up the dirt to the noses
Of the white horses. And water began falling
From the sky. "I will show you how to touch
The earth. I will show you how to die.
Eric Garner Emmett Till Freddie Gray
Korryn Gaines Trayvon Martin Martin Luther
King El-Hajj Malik Shabazz Fred Hampton
Kalief Browder Sandra Bland Rumain Brisbon
Akai Gurley Tamir Rice Laquan McDonald
Kajieme Powell Ezell Ford Dante Parker
Michael Brown John Crawford Tyree Woodson
Victor White Yvette Smith McKenzie Cochran
Jordan Baker Andy Lopez Miriam
Carey Jonathon Ferrell Carlos Alcis

Larry Jackson Kimani Gray Rekia Boyd
Malissa Williams Timothy Russell
Reynaldo Cuevas Chavis Carter Shantel Davis
Henry Dumas Sharmel Edwards Shereese Francis
Wendell Allen Deion Fludd. Flood. Flood.

"Flood. The gates of the cemetery
Are now open." A great tumult started:
Water, the clanging of machetes, and the boy,
My namesake, heading up into the limbs of a tree . . .

SOMETHING ABOUT JOHN COLTRANE

Something about a tree in shallow sleep
Listening for what it wants to remember:

The note of a seed, its neck sliding through
Dirt and its confusion—nothing cleansed

Of struggle. The weight lost after death,
A confrontation of death. John Coltrane

Even in death is a perfect instrument
Of water and working the day past its zero—

The fires in the trees, a *legless rabbit*
Drifting across the sky—dream of a mule

Covered in crows opened in front of a mule
Covered in crows, their wings beating against him

Like skin. An autumned tree in autumn
Watching fire autumn the other trees.

It doesn't have to make sense now; it can
Make sense later on. A mule covered in crows—

Sometimes, you got to stick a little grass
In your mouth to sound like God. Allow crows.

Something about John Coltrane

Something about the bells in a faun's hair,
A black boy standing in the rain at the edge

Of the road, wondering how to cross it
Without summoning his death or its hand-

Maidens, the grasshoppers clicking against him
Like he's the water the world has been meaning

To come to—all the world's water trapped inside
Him and needing to be let out. Something

About water waking a ghost, and the ghost
waking a seed, rain in the hair of the world,

And the world opening its sudden flesh
The way stone opens sound against it—a bridge

Thrown from one absence to another,
As if to say, *Extinction, I can live there too.*

Something about Marion Brown

In a Georgia afternoon, the faun listens
To the Holy Ghost in a trickle of water

And is suddenly thrown down on the floor
Of the Sanctified Church, the woman's feet

Lifting, stomping against the wooden boards,
And God somewhere he ain't supposed to be

Or be momentarily, wasp in the hedge
Sheltering from the rain; a woman's skirt

Hoisted and gladdened above her knee, the hem,
The hem of her garment touched by the faun's eye

And holy, holy, holy is thy name and the snow
The woman becomes on the floor and the water

Ticking against the bottom of the pail, and, Lord,
The bridge opening above the faun in the air,

And he is what memory permits—pine needles
Turning on the skin of a bucket of water,

A bare shoulder in the rain,
God somewhere he ain't supposed to be.

Something about Marion Brown

When the light came to the Georgia faun,
It was in a trickle of water, a brown leaf

Suddenly underfoot in the spring's ringing
Green, the leaf underfoot spoke, speaks, became

A ladder of tongues—ghost and the good wood
A house fire needs—*yes, good God, good God yes—*

Became the pleasure of placing your mouth—
Oh yes, Lord, right here, right now Lord—on something

Holy and holding it there until every
Sound in you becomes water—water moving

Over stone, moving in the hair of the trees,
Moving over the breast of the bee, beaver,

Buck of the day, its brown shoulder bearing
The hesitant light, its crown and thorn, water

Moving over the infinite gates of the city,
Moving as the wing of the wasp, which is

The voice of God, water moving over the two
Realms of the body, moving as the name of God—

Something is coming to kill him,
And something is coming to be born.

Today, he is both. Something beyond blood.
Wasp somewhere in the hedge sheltering from the rain.

Something about Aretha Franklin

Cousin Mary, don't weep. The eternal
Without the wound of eternity begins now.

Sometimes, you can be made more   than your body
While still in your body. Now, that's power—

A dog suddenly crying in the stables
For no other reason than something lifted

In him in the afternoon, lifted way up
And shook him into a moan and blade of grass

Gathered by a gale wind into a speaking
Thing. Just ask the Georgia faun all caught up

In some running and gladdened by it. Happy
Is what the old folks say. The boy, happy,

Happying in the field with nothing more
Than his body and the dark landing its dark

Against him. It doesn't have to make sense now.
It can make sense later on. The faun coming

In the rain. The dark bending about him.
Power, Cousin Mary, power in the faun

Climbing into the tree as the dark earth flying.
And the clouds coming together above him,

And no danger, no danger to hanging
In the lower heavens as a bell,

As foreign pollen breaking in the wind,
Scattering its brown voice on anything

That will bear and not bear its gold. Vine, Fence,
A pail of water, the exposed shoulders of God.

Now, that's power, Cousin Mary. And nothing
Dying rudely or for a dream of the rood.

The dream of this tree is not what will die
In it but what will live upside down

In the rain, trying its voice in heaven
And on earth. Power, eternal power,

Cousin Mary. Don't weep.

Something about the Dream of a Tree

Something about a mule covered in crows,
The mule ridden by a faun with bells in his hair,

And the boy ringing across the field,
And the field ringing across the boy,

And all this ringing opening and with
And full of and tarrying and the silk skin of

And glory and the hem of a garment and *Help me,
Holy Ghost* and *yes, Lord, yes* and *the tiny racket*

A seed makes cracking open in the dark and the stone
In the field worshipping the field by letting

The day fall all about it without moving,
And the dusk riding the rain and the tree

Dreaming and the light, the light without
Confession, castigation or beauty

But beauty, and the faun thrown down
In memory of once watching a hawk

Plucking red coins from the breast of a squirrel,
And the faun mimicking the hawk, his head

Dipping forward in the gesture of prayer,
His mouth working against the wind, the invisible

Breast and belly of an animal and the seed
Of something opening inside him

For which there was no source so call it mercy,
Grace, or nothing   but becoming power.

Prayer. Hawk. The dream of a tree . . .

          The dream, also an autopsy—
What came in the middle of the night, a tree

Muttering about the muddle of fragrance,
Wounded sky *bewound in light*, morning

Misted in murder, maggots chattering
Dawn's red rousing, calling it milk,

My Cherie Amour's mystic wobble—
The autopsy, also a dream—what came:

A boy who found his work on the road
And had to lie down there with his work—

The hostility of living between the bullets
And the bullets hanging you against the night,

By the lapel, for examination, for a song,
For the smiths of gold, for gold, for the gallows,

For the fragrance of a field covered in crows
And the crows lifting as if a great black tent

Rising to shield the field from pestilence
But the crows just rising crows, the fragrance

Of freedom but not freedom itself—and here
Silence, what came in the middle of the night—

An autopsy, a dream: a boy on the road,
Crows bowing and bowing and bowing to the dead.

Something about Michael Brown

Something about Mahalia Jackson's wig,
The crow and angel of it, its closer-

Walk-with-Jesus, with-thee, satisfied, lonely,
Holy, ghost, blessed in rapture, actual

And otherwise, her wig, a walking on water
With the faith of a wig; each wave of black hair

A pew strapped to the forehead of prayer
And singing all in it. What's it all about

Is burning beyond loss, learning to rise
In and out of disaster smelling of smoke

That can heal the sick—wild cathedral
In the wilderness opening itself

To any light, dream, or dram of song unhitched
From heaven; And the mules and men get so happy,

Hallelujahed, they strut, brown-suited, bewound
In light like bow-legged Louis Armstrong

At the Newport Jazz Festival, 1970, Mahalia
Lining out ECSTASY and sweating through it

Until it can do nothing but rain
And the second line, confused, leaf-strewn, late,

Limps onto stage, but Mahalia Jackson's wig
Keeps flying, and the rain touches evening's brow

Bringing with it the stars and Mahalia
Jackson's wig flying as if a star

Suddenly freed from the mouth of God
A Black tooth blessing. No longer, no longer

Shall you take things second or third hand—joy

Ecstasy, pleasure, the blessing of sitting in the rain
While gathered in the hair of some tree—

Because Mahalia Jackson's wig is flying,
And the dead, for once, are dancing, too—in the rain.

ODE TO PABLO NERUDA'S "ODE TO A LEMON"

"Out of lemon flowers loosed on the moonlight,"
Me touching the "barbarous gold" with my mouth—

"The breast and nipple." To fall into the world as this
Yellow clamoring of God—is this not ecstasy—

Lying in bed with ink, book, and lemons,
Mouth to the lemons, to ink, me, lashed and lashed

By a poet whose revenge against the State is cutting
Open a piece of yellow fruit slowly in front of it;

The juice, in its bizarre light and running
Along the Senate floor, is the exile's homeland

Beyond burning and exile. "The harbors
Are big with it." Death hangs fire at the water's edge

Ready to become a field of smoke with you in it,
But there in your pocket, a lemon and a knife—

The rind pierced, the sound of which is a statehouse
Burning, ash without its requisite singing. Now sing.

RICH BLACK, OR BEST BARBARIAN

When our consent was against our will
As in "It is said during slavery
    Negro children were encumbrances

    Often advertised in evening papers" as lagniappe
The petite largesse of luxury living
    As in "Scipio baptized 1760 likely Negro boy

    About a month old to be given away"
Into the sea as in below the harbor
    Near Edisto Island Igbos swung low

    In the chariot of their calling to be
Carried home and walked
    On the bottom of water until handsome homed

    As in *the way we lay we mimed a body of water*
So died for the want of water
    Bearing this plow and flower

    This bit and scold's bridle this mule-ing
Leather this blood lost
    This goodbye gone

    But one gone ain't always equivalent to another
As in all silences are not the same
    As in all money ain't good money

What silences are you responsible for
What Jims have you jiggered
    Into crows cajoled to sing in the pines

    And pages of poetry magazines for a prize
As in there is no succinct definition of exile
    As in Black is the Black ain't

    As in everywhere the bucks went clattering
The police bristled in the way
    As in form forgets fugitivity is the original human

    Form as in best put on your best barbarian
As in this gospel is large enough
    That anything can be said about *me and you*

    Your momma and your cousin too
Rolling down the strip on Vogues
    Waking up slamming Cadillac doors Outkast

    And out of gas the empire smiles in its guillotine
And Gucci loafers
    As if to say 'I practice the abundance of zero'

    As in the world is always ending
While someone is and ain't
    Being born as in motherfuck the weather

    Come and join the band of wild negroes
Dancing the antelope and Holy Ghost
    In Gadsden Gethsemane and Georgia

As in leave the angel to his centuries
Of death leave the police dog
Of our future in his heavy paws

Below the "Whites Only" signs and water fountains
Dreaming of bucks
Between his teeth and a healthy 401K

Or Roth IRA to ease into old age
And the arthritis of chasing
Everywhere the bucks go clattering

As in the black and blur or the bright blur of black
As in the negro must be still
Must still be moving which is the original

Cinematic motion of ghosts gardens and ex-slaves
As in address yourself only to freedom
To the seed the forest the swamp the night

The rain the river the rat the snake
The panther the tree
Leaping in and out of its green breath

Lord, let me be useful, and not
The green jaguar stitched in the cross-
Hairs of some night vision scope
Meant to hush me into the uncut
Kitchen of an inconsiderate lawn,
My hushing a gust of bells excited,
Gonging, just long enough for the oligarch
Hunter to raise my head to his,
Pluck my eyes from their sockets, and forget
Them in his pockets until airport security
Demands he empty what's concealed,
Pull out his forgetfulness for full
Inspection, not this wicked-flame
Animal fire caught in the draft
Of a slamming door, innuendo of an end
Whistling its horror in my ribs
And kidneys until the blood lets and ladders
The ghost down into the heart
And bile of its disappearance and walks
Out to where the other ghosts shimmy-
Shimmy and slip out of the trees and tea
Cups broken at the bottom of war,
The baker's one-armed son half-way home
Returning in the mouth of a white tiger
Moon, all balanced on the back of a wagon
That signs and sings its creaky complaint,
I have slept, I have slept the sleep of reason.
Here, here, are my monsters. Now let me
Sleep, let me sleep. Lord, not this, not this, but,

Lord, let me be that other miraculous
Instrument, the night's leopard rebuking its god-
Given golden fur, embracing the hush
Of its spots in the tall grass, the hunter
Unaware that when he raises the head
Of the dead animal to his chest and the camera
I, Lord, I am coming with my mouth
Open, my mouth, Lord, ready to fang
And tear wherever my hunger falls upon him.
Lord, let me be the golden heaven rising
Above him, the hush of a slamming door.

DRAPETOMANIA, OR JAMES BALDWIN AS AN IMPROVISATION

Absent bounty, anarchic and asymptotic,
Bedlam banked as beauty, captive cuckolding
Capital and its camel-faced captor, master, the
Devil is in the dove's details, even doves
Exist as furious, fragile, violent and decent
(Which could describe anyone at all, including
Freedom), even freedom exists, god's good
Hostage, haint haunting the hootenanny,
If, as in the *if-only-you-knew* of Patti
LaBelle sung in the broken-bottle falsetto
Of an uncle laid out on the bottom step
Of summer, sobriety, and Miss Such-
A-Much's sliding-away love, jaundiced
As James Baldwin's good and lovely dying

Eye; James Baldwin existed as an improvisation,
Knuckles calling for a Newport to knock, light,
Lift, lustrous and otherwise, Malcom X
Marking X where it is he loved the poor—
Everywhere, everywhere, which is where
Detroit is red, recalcitrant, panther,
Battlefield where the moon says I love you,
Naysayers, narcoleptics, no-names, nap-
Deprived, on time and out of time, queer—
The color of how we made it over empire,
Petulance, pneumonia, the nubs, neck pain,
Needles nosing in our nana's uterus,
Notices of eviction, *Notes on the State
Of Virginia* and how negroes ain't shit

But buckra-beaters, bears, butches, bull-
Daggers and welfare queens, sometimes, cute,
Coons, country, cow-tipped, downward dogs, earth-
Empty, flies, fungible, freaks, gutter-rough,
Hasslers, hijinks, handsome in harnesses,
Ignorant as ice, juridical conundrums
Nappy kitchens, kaput, light and heavy
Work, madness's martyr and minor
Mayhem, misled Drapetomaniacs,
Nothing worth noting, a now made then,
Occult and organized as outlandish,
Pariahs, presidents, quarrelsome,
Roustabouts and randy, skit, scat, and shat,
Tercentennial and tough-going

Mulattoes, tragic and otherwise,
Translated as any number of ain'ts,
Apocalypses, unaffiliated
And unctuous, various and varicose,
Vestibules of the new world—remnants
Of light from a cigarette balanced
Between the knuckles of James Baldwin's hand,
Leopard, the remnants of light exist,
Wayward as any many and less
Where the moon fields the night, and the shadow
Of a boy running through an unplowed field
Turns the earth, turns the earth round, gold,
Back against the bedlam of being hunted by any
X, Y, and Z; you, you who survived this earth.

GRENDEL'S MOTHER

It was not like the woman who had come out of hell,
Haired and furred in black earth, smelling of fire,
Her lover, green and brown in the green and brown
Field, his back a torn limb broken from the tree
Of her; ripped, the gesture of his uneven walking,
His refusal to turn to her who called to him,
Mouthing the 'Or-, 'Or- of his name,
As if she were giving his wading away
From her through the tall grass a counter
Offer, argument—*Me, turn, turn to me, to us,*
And in that leaving gesture of a ripped limb,
He turned to her, to *us*, and even the ram
Who drove his skull into the rocks stopped
His thinking and watched the woman yanked
Back down into the earth's black holler
And soil, and so was outside of thinking,
So furious. So furious, I was,
When my son called to me, called me out of heaven
To come to the crag and corner store
Where it was that he was dying, *Mama,
I can't breathe*; even now I hear it—the limb
Of him broken in the black beast-bird's morning
Call that pins the heaven to the black road.
I can't breathe in the water's curve and slur
Over the narrow paths, in the trail and gutter
His body made in the mud, where the sky
Barges in and fills. It was not like the woman
Who had come out of hell, *Orpheus*
Unable to touch her. I touched my son

In his dying, where he was crushed, cairn,
Blood-belt of the dying earth and without
Song other than my feet shuffling in the dead
Leaves, which is not the song I wanted
To give to his dying, to his dark
And darkening ear. The day opening,
Sun warming stone and the musk of it,
Where the river-flowers bleed their yellow
Scent on the water, *Ever,* even *Ever*
In its any and always, in its absence
Of meekness, which is to say, God—I wanted
For him a hunger outside of heaven.

"ESPÍRITU SANTO TAMBIÉN . . ."

If "the naked human body is the grave in blossom,"
What is the dressed body of the dead—you,

Seed, caught in the cuff of a blue casket? What tree?
What door, what rose, what morning, what black milk,

What bandage discarded in a field? Have you climbed
The braid of God yet and touched his head, his injured mouth?

What does he say of all of this misery on the ground,
Here, our reticence to do anything about it?

Look at me here like the children in that one-tree
Field stomping on those dead wooden doors,

Their heels making a silence rise over the hacked head
Of the sun and calling it noise. Love. What silence am I

Making rise? What stutter? How can I make you stay, you
Who now have everything, you, the blood, mouth, and ghost of God?

"Do I long for my virginity?" Sappho asks from the fragments,
From the sun-bright blades and horns of dawn clattering on the floor,

From inside a tomb, her office now the old heaven of pleasure
Where a god that had been ignored can be called down

With its spears and oblivion to a couch or field and submit
A body, a lover, to the distress of love, and the god comes

Because gods, too, need and are lonely and are generally unneeded
Except in matters that cannot be mastered which are most

Matters and the shadow of those matters from which you call,
Sappho: "Do I long for my virginity?" Why, why

Sappho, this marble beneath my tongue, this shadow, this stone
Across my face, this thirty-year memory spreading out

Over me as if I could forget its claws, confusion, its flashing bells,
And violation? The virtue . . . the virtue of violation—*Is there no end?*

Is there no end to the bed, the wall, her hand
Across six-year-old young mouth, her hand

Plummeting me like a stone, like a stone I did not want
Her across and down and against me;

Is there no end, no way to drive this from me—
Me, arriving, bewildered, boy, naked below the waist

In the dark, untouched, forever awaiting a touch?
Do I long for my virginity, Sappho?

Confession: I long, I square, I male, I roach,
I thing, I cock, I crawl, I hair and hair all over the stairs

Unable to give a precise account of my virginity
Or where, where is the end of speaking to the dead

Of the brutal obligations of memory? Where, where
Is the end to this being of who I was, who I am?

Who will—waking me from the dark, from dawn—yell
"Roger, Roger, you are yet alive and mostly, mostly free"?

I've come to this headless finch
Tangled in sunlight and kudzu vine
Along the Raritan, just off the river
General Washington boated and prowled
With the teeth of former slaves in his head
To place my body in the way
Of something other than my death,
But even Orpheus couldn't manage this,
The Maenads tossing his head into a river,
The head singing into its dismembered oblivion.
A sheaf of wheat blown from a graveyard
Into the foyer of an elementary school
And the hum of a truck's tread
That sought to crush me flat as Gilgamesh's sacred lute
Crow and crowd my running head,
But I'm fortunate to have a buffalo's patience
For finding water in a jaundiced plain
And a woman who can drive an angel out
Of me or a gazelle's skin stretched over a log.
I know the ascension of dragging a lake
For a tenor's tongue and watching a body
Descend and rise into a parade of clay and bells.
I come from a land where a dead hog stretched out
Over a picnic table means good harvest
And we only lost one child to a tree,
The head sweetening the pines
Into a night of shifting chants . . .
O song of the river blood, o blood of the river song . . .
I pawned my box of precious medicines
For a bottle of brown liquor, rent money,

And several mink coats. I envy the sea
Turtle's ability to be at home while traveling
In and out of exile, in and out of the blood
Salting the ocean and paradise.
There is no terror like this: making a soul
Out of the sound of your aunt hanging from a joist
In the middle of a barn, her lashed gashes
Produced and reproduced like a Gershwin tune—
I loves you Porgy . . . I loves you Porgy . . .
There is no terror like this: running along the Raritan,
Watching snakes climb out of the water
And run through the forest like men.

PAST BARABBAS

The funeral past, and also I loved him.
And also I, him, and so loved past him.
And so all funeral the past ran animal
Up to our eyes, and so, lo, I loved
Any which him, the I-him, the scandal-
Animal of him hanging his newborn
Twenty years past newborn out of a moving car,
The silence of the road sorrowing up.
I didn't want to begin with music,
The hack and rasp of shovels, the hiss of white
Chairs tallying the fraudulence and broken
Hip of my uncle already five days
Past Barabbas, the shekels spent on Hen-
Nessy, the account drained, thieved, drained,
My father, seven days in silence, God
Touching his weariness (or not) like a hunter
That comes upon a broken instrument
In the woods, the thing made feral
By its brokenness so cautiously he attends
To the gut and tender of it, his hand
Raising the neck from the leaves, running one
Finger across its throat and listening
For blood or what blood remains howling. Wolf.

XXX

When your mother finds you, over-
Dressed for death in that rat-shit
Apartment, oven-roasted and over-
Dosed on a serpent that promised
Night without shadow or shouting,
Shouting without a valley to echo
Its eventual and awfully uneventful
End, I was standing in a canyon
Being bit by horseflies in the mouth
Of a cave that hurried darkness
Over the afternoon and after.
Somewhere in a valley, a boy
Finds himself holding the head of snake
Wondering if bit will he turn
Into a bull or a woman,
As he's been told by the local preacher.
He's fine with both just as long as
He doesn't have to become an angel
Assigned to wrestling aggrieved and anxious
Men who haunt hills and burning bushes
For blessings. A story rarely closes
Without a good singeing or singing;
A snake in the palm and the heel
Bitten. In the mouth of flies, I make
A joyful noise. Your head
In your mother's hand makes
A joyful noise that none of us can hear.

Sometimes, one death will cover another
As singing can cover singeing
As a mother can cover her son
In a blaze of Hallelujahs
None of us hear over the night
Gowning and galloping out her grief.
The horseflies at the window
Want to leave the poem. They want down
Into the valley with the boy
Who has become a bull, black,
Glistening, mouth working a noise
Over wild amaranth. Agreed
To be drawn to blood, they beg me,
To let them go away from here, never
Wanting to be possessed by anything
Other than their hunger. But like you,
My blood, in the soft bulb of their bellies,
Calls to me without language
But full of need. Your blood, Blood, my blood,
Blood, is in the valley of the mortician's bowl
Yea, though I walk the canyon in the mouth
Of flies, yea, though you haunt the dark hills
And your mother, my mother in the pews
Sounding like a bush on fire—the poverty
That is the end to every story—the road
The maggots will travel to churn your body into milk.

LEAF-SIGH AND BRAY

I mistake the end of *Paradise*
For the end of *Jazz*. The end
Of your thigh against mine
As the end of applause—
Ecstasy has but one name,
But boy can it mumble
Raising several poems from the grass
And none of them graves
Though lightning, though fire,
Though wreck, though blood
Though God takes off his hat
And allows the world its solstice
Of pain, the scarred sky, Us
In it. Are we beneath flesh?
Have we turned inward
Toward each other yet
Where *ecstasy is more leaf-sigh*
Than bray; and, no matter
Where the sycamore bends
It is always touching itself
Even in the maul of a saw
So very far from itself
It is itself wholly,
Wholly—you in the grain of me
As I walk beneath a sycamore
Whose leaves are turning the color of blood
On an evening turning the color of blood.

How else shall I carry the abyss
Between us other than as fire,
As the mistake the sycamore makes
Entering the burning-down door of the saw?

"And on the third day, Jesus said, 'rise up and walk,'"
Said my father, dead now for more than three days.
He walked and walked and walked. Over to me,
On the side of my grandmother's house, the grass green
As it has always been even in the shadows,
And the shadows playing with the conversation
Of the day, and the apple of knowledge
Had made its appearance but no longer on the tree,
Just in the conversation of art and who was
Alive in it, then he showed up, my father,
From behind me, as if I birthed him from the tree of my back,
The shadow it made within the shadow of the house,
And I fell and was suddenly in a lawn of yellow light.
Not a column, not a column of light—a gift—
A golden column of light in winter
Touching the stubble of a priest's face
Caught in the black doorway of a church
As he was coming out into the cold winter street—
A gift. It was not a gift, though down in the pig,
In the pig of that light, I asked how, how
Had he come back. And no one would answer
Me. Not my companions, who once spoke
Wildly of the total bewilderment of darkness,
The insane sovereignty of winter,
Rain. My companions now mute as light,
Stubble on a sleeping man's face. In that light,
Thrown down in light, I asked my father how

He had come back, and he would not answer me
Other than to say: "On the third day, Jesus
Said, 'rise up and walk.'" Thus, this, the third day
Of his death—the gift of being thrown down in light.

AS A CHILD OF NORTH AMERICA

And Abraham lifted up his eyes, and looked, and behold behind him a
ram caught in a thicket by his horns: and Abraham went and took the
ram, and offered him up for a burnt offering in the stead of his son.

—GENESIS 22:13

I wept for the ram and was told not to—
His life—in the thicket, horn-held and groped
By thorn and God, stone table and knife—his
Life—crazed for sure, a free animal
Until master, mastery, and the Lord
Grants his vision—capture—the ram's flesh
Chattering, smoke covering the face of God.
I was told to celebrate this vision—
The tambourine knocked and fluttering
Against the heel of my mother's hand
Drove the smoke higher—and higher the church
Climbed to witness the smoke, the ram,
A burning angel burning in the eye of God,
And God wild as the eye of a goat
Watching its body walk out from beneath it
In prophecy, in flame. *How does it feel*
To be a problem, my mother once asked
From behind a knife and the first ten years of a century
Whose last ten years will resemble a goat
Hemmed in thorns, awaiting a knife, a new century to die
In. *How does it feel to be a problem?*
I answer upon a stone table, conscripted
By tambourine and its talons drawing me higher,
Higher until I am what vision forgets—

Something thrashing, a second sun of blood
Coming out of the day's slow thighs,
Mismanaged mercy so silent. I would remind you
I did not coo into the knife, I did not coo
Though I wept like a goat and was glad.

What shall be done with the demand
For more selfies, selfies of the crow
In the wheat and the wheat knocking

Against the window, selfies of my daughter
Hooting like an owl and beating
The back of her cage, the back of her bones,

Selfies of Wittgenstein's eyes
Settling on the back of a crow
Which is the shadow of a boy

Delivering milk to the door of his mother—
Where language began, begins—
Gertrude Stein over the Steinbauergasse

Eating salt-fish and conch fritters
With Aimé Césaire, more selfies of negroes
From Niger and Nor'leans, blue-black

In the blue-black buck and canter of summer
In Yves Saint Laurent glasses and pinafores
Of light pinned to the eyes—no church in the wild,

But more selfies of Susie Asado buck-dancing
On balustrades near the nigger
Cemeteries where the chariots swung so low

We just called them commas—we
'bout to fuck up some commas yeah—
Gerrymander and Jack Johnson the shit

Out of shit—why do white women
Love black men—"because we eat
Cold eels and think distant thoughts."

Jack Johnson—we need more selfies—
Selfies of Frederick Douglass's pen
Removed from the gashes in his feet

And writing hot checks for Rolexes and rivers
Our bodies just can't cash—wade
In the water, wade in the water, children—

We 'bout to fuck up some trauma, yeah—
Selfie and holler yeah, Instagram at the ashram
With Lil' Weezy and Wardell Curry, Junior

Not Senior, bustin' three pointers, yeah,
On behalf of a local charity that sends mosquito
Nets to children in Africa, the Sudan—

Niger—I don't know—Tyger
Tyger burning bright! Tyger
Tyger hanging from the street light! —Distant thought:

I'm so in time I'm outta time—so selfie
I'm healthy—I mean I'm sayin though
You know what I'm sayin—

BY BEAUTY, FROM BEYOND THE VOICE OF GOD

Sha-clack-clack and all the black black,
We free singers be south of success,
East of gloss, a black wedding song

Lost in its singing of loss, the next
Beauty broken by beauty—
This love is a rich cry over,

A bone to bear on bare bones,
A golden yell, heaven hurt
Past hurt, which is the earth restored

Of its mercy, the coyote
Given the deer and the dead rabbit,
The dead given their sudden death.

God this freedom is difficult
Especially when doing it
Without a deranging and dead God.

.   .   .

Sha-clack-clack—it was like that moment in the subway—you remember—when
the police surrounded the man—"one of the police got behind him, on his knees,
the other—like little boys—pushed him over. They did that, and somehow the
nightstick hit the pavement," which means a God had fallen.

"So here come the other police. They didn't ask questions," their faith in God, in the nightstick fallen. "They formed a ring around him and tried to hit him with their sticks, but they couldn't hit him"—because God had fallen.

"He moved his head about and moved his head about. They surrounded him, and all at once, he said, "Creator, help me!" And then this voice came out of nowhere and said, "Leave the motherfucker alone!" So now, they stopped and looked around. They saw nothing, but they didn't continue" because something beyond the voice of God had spoken, something beyond the live and dead nettle, something for which there was no source, which means something beyond beauty but not its report.

YOUR HAND TO YOUR FACE BLOCKING THE SUN

Became a revelation
    As the pear tree is a revelation to itself each spring

    It sitting in the dead of itself and making something
That which we will call pear

    Though was nothing more than water and a little ache in the branches
A moan of white flowers
        Rocking the green river of a tree until full

        Ache
  A revelation
        Unaccompanied by the requisite panic

        Me along the curve of you
            A flower's moan
        So inelegant

    It will be mistaken for dirt flung into the eyes
        A broken door opening
Newport knocked and floating on a puddle's gray rose
        Which is how a man might describe something he loves
That will kill him

        Is that how we move
When we move upon each other

As if whatever is leaving
    Is the prayer we've been meaning to come to

106

I CAN DRINK THE DISTANCE, OR FIRE IN THE LAKE

"As a stone in love" with falling, I "wound
The water's face" then wear the mask of water,

Wounding all the way down into the lake.
The distance of my falling remains a loss,

An abyss I've consented to so arrive,
I arrive, not as thought but as some angel

Of derangement—failure, however brief,
Success—my flesh, fire in the lake, loss

Lost—it's as if now I understand Lucifer
For the first time, cast out, still naked in the grass,

And for the first time, the grass appearing as the grass
Because there was something burning in it,

Risking to be seen. Prophet propheting
Prophecy. The un-civilizing work of vision

And rising above vision. Neither awaiting a flame
Stolen from a God nor awaiting a God

Stolen from a flame. For once, love
Not as illumination but illumination itself.

Alice Coltrane, her harp, fills in the cracks of me
With gold. The Japanese call it Kintsugi.
Where the vessel broken, only gold will permit
Its healing. Its history. It's *How the Stars Understand
Us*, lemon flowers on the skin of the earth,
Mosquito filled with the blood that sirens its fat,
Long life. Who isn't dying to leave this house,
To go masked only in the shadow of one's animal-
Breathing, lonesome, unprotected, *knowing
Nothing lives as foreignness* or death,
That the black dog with the sword in his mouth
Passing from house to house will not bring its itch,
Its ticks and locks clogging our lungs, a permanent
Quarantine—nothing that a little gold
Melted to ichor and spilled into the veins
Won't seam. Everything is a blue divergence
On a harp, the red bells in the purple
Crepe myrtle this morning forgetting
That soon they will be the corpses the spring
Tree kneels to observe. No, no, they remember,
As everything dying remembers its mother's
Name. *Say your mother's name.* Not for power
But for the glimpse of power, to be more
Than a hesitation, gold filling in the cracks,
A window thrown open for no other reason
Than to continue a blue feeling, nothing
Needed other than this devotion to darkness,
A Fire Gotten Brighter, my daughter holding
My small name in her mouth, light-broken

Beloved, my daughter—a window thrown
Open—her voice, gold filling in the cracked
Basketball court of me, announcing *all*
Nature, all nature will be dead for life soon.

FOR BLACK CHILDREN AT THE END OF THE WORLD—AND THE BEGINNING

You are in the black car burning beneath the highway
And rising above it—not as smoke

But what causes it to rise. Hey, Black Child,
You are the fire at the end of your elders'

Weeping, fire against the blur of horse, hoof,
Stick, stone, several plagues including time.

Chrysalis hanging on the bough of this night
And the burning world: *Burn, Baby, burn.*

Anvil and iron be thy name, yea though ye may
Walk among the harnessed heat and huntsmen

Who bear their masters' hunger for paradise
In your rabbit-death, in the beheading of your ghost.

You are the healing snake in the heather
Bursting forth from your humps of sleep.

In the morning, your tongue moves along the earth
Naming hawk sky; rabbit run; your tongue,

Poison to the filthy democracy, to the gold-
Domed capitols where the Guard in their grub-

Worm-colored uniforms cling to the blades of grass—
Worm on the leaf, worm in the dust, worm,

Worm made of rust: sing it with me,
Dragon of Insurmountable Beauty.

Black Child, laugh at the men with their hoofs
and borrowed muscle, their long and short guns,

The worm of their faces, their casket ass-
Embling of the afternoon, left over leaves

From last year's autumn scrapping across their boots;
Laugh, laugh at their assassins on the roofs

(For the time of the assassin is also the time of hysterical laughter).

Black Child, you are the walking-on-of-water
Without the need of an approving master.

You are in a beautiful language.

You are what lies beyond this kingdom
And the next and the next and fire. Fire, Black Child.

ACKNOWLEDGMENTS

American Poetry Review
"Something About John Coltrane"

Baffler
"I Can Drink the Distance" | "Without the Pelt of a Lion"

Believer
"Cocaine and Gold" | "Future"

The Best American Poetry 2021
"For Black Children at the End of the World—and the Beginning"

Five Points
"As a Child of North America" | "Cyclops and Balthazar" | "Leaf-Sigh and Bray" |
"Poem, In an Old Language"

Gulf Coast
"Into the West"

Kenyon Review
"Fragment 107" | "Rich Black, or Best Barbarian" | "Sovereign Silence, or The City"

Los Angeles Review of Books
"so, Ecstasy" (I and II)

Nation
"Echo: From the Mountains"

New Republic
"American Runner" | "Ode to Pablo Neruda's 'Ode to a Lemon'"

The New Yorker
"Grendel" | "Standing in the Atlantic"

Northwest Review
"Mother's Day"

Paris Review
"American Landscaping, Philadelphia to Mount Vernon"

Ploughshares
"After the Funeral"

Plume
"Your Hand to Your Face Blocking the Sun"

Poem-a-Day
"Children Listen"
"For Black Children at the End of the World—and the Beginning"

Poetry
"Domestic Violence"

Pushcart Prize XLIV: Best of the Small Presses, 2020
"American Landscaping, Philadelphia to Mount Vernon"

Sewanee Review
"Caught in a Black Doorway" | "Grendel's Mother" | "Journey to Satchidananda"

Tin House
"Past Barabbas" | "Prayer of the Jaguar"

Virginia Quarterly Review
"The Alphabet, for Naima" | "Drapetomania, or James Baldwin As an Improvisation"

Yale Review
"After Death" | "Rat Among the Pines"

NOTES

"WITHOUT THE PELT OF A LION"

The title of this poem riffs off of the first line of David Ferry's "to where" and also calls to his translation of the *Aeneid*.

"THE ALPHABET, FOR NAIMA"

"the shy speechless sound of fruit falling from its tree" is from Ossip Mandelstam's "Stone," translated by W. S. Merwin and Clarence Brown.

"would make the petals fall" is from Gwendolyn Brooks's "A Lovely Love"

"IN REHEARSAL FOR THE FUNERAL"

This poem is after David Ferry and Arthur Gold. I also quote a line from Ferry's "Reading Arthur Gold's Poem 'Rome, December 1973'": "a forgotten destination not yet known." The title, too, is a partial quotation of a line. The full line reads: "In rehearsal for the funeral later on."

"INTO THE WEST"

The opening quote is from *The Confessions of St. Augustine.*

"THE BROKEN FIELDS MENDED"

The epigraph comes from Walt Whitman's "Song of Myself," section 17.

"SO, ECSTASY"

The line "made into the vessel that which must be made" is from Frank Bidart's "As the Eye to the Sun" in *Desire.*

"CYCLOPS AND BALTHAZAR"

"Like a veil across the stars" is quoted from Langston Hughes's "Let America Be America Again."

"MOTHER'S DAY"

The phrase "the wind resting its cheek on the ground" is from the first line of James Schuyler's "Hymn to Life."

"POEM, IN AN OLD LANGUAGE"

"tongue of flame" and "crowned knot of fire" are from T. S. Eliot's "Little Giddings" in the *Four Quartets*. In "Little Giddings," it is "tongues of flame," but I want to be ethical and accurate in my citation work.

"THE END OF GHASSAN KANAFANI"

"Is this peace not a conversation between the sword and the neck" is a riff off of a response Ghassan Kanafani, a writer and political leader for Popular Front for the Liberation of Palestine, gave to reporter Richard Carleton in 1970 when he asked why the Popular Front didn't sit down with Israeli leaders. Kanafani responded that that conversation was not only futile but impossible, because "that is the kind of conversation between the sword and the neck." Kanafani was responding to Carleton casting the Palestinian liberation movement as a "conflict" or "civil war," as opposed to what it was—a people seeking to get out from under colonization and discrimination. Footage of the interview is available on YouTube: https://www.youtube.com/watch?v=3h_drCmG2iM.

"DOMESTIC VIOLENCE"

This poem converses with and riffs away from Dante Alighieri's *Inferno*, Geoffrey Chaucer's *Parliament of Fowls*, Book Six of Virgil's *Aeneid*, Ezra Pound's *Pisan Cantos*, and Gwendolyn Brooks's "Anniad."

When Ezra Pound enters the poem, he says, "He do the police in different voices," which was the title of T. S. Eliot's "The Waste Land" before Pound, in his editing, suggested Eliot retitle the poem. "Domestic Violence" also alludes to Pound's time in Pisa, where he was arrested for treason just after Allied Forces took control of Italy.

"The prince hanging by his heels in the piazza" refers to Benito Mussolini, the fascist dictator of Italy, whose body was dragged through the streets after he was shot in the northern Italian city of Giulino di Mezzegra, and later hanged. Pound refers to him as a "prince" throughout the *Pisan Cantos*, ten sections of Pound's larger work the *Cantos*. Pound wrote the *Pisan Cantos* during his time as an American prisoner in Italy. It also happens that Pound was imprisoned with Emmett Till's father, Louis Till. Yes, that Emmett Till. In fact, Louis Till makes an appearance in the *Pisan Cantos* on multiple occasions. Pound refers to him as "St. Louis" because he, along with the other Black soldiers, treated Pound well. Louis Till's hanging by the US military is also memorialized in the *Pisan Cantos*. Pound writes, "and Till was hung yesterday..."

Louis Till's guides in the afterlife are the poets Audre Lorde, Gwendolyn Brooks, and Lucille Clifton. They speak as one. In "Domestic Violence," their speech is built through the amalgamation of several of their poems. For instance, "I is the total black" comes from Lorde's "Coal," and the syntax of "The god-head-glitter-gussied-up-for-the-going-down" mimics Brooks's "Anniad." There are also poetic citations and citational nods to the work of Clifton.

"We started from the bottom, now here" is borrowed from Drake's "Started from the Bottom."

Oya is the orisha of the cemetery in the Yoruba religion.

"SOMETHING ABOUT JOHN COLTRANE"

This poem takes its inspiration from jazz artist Alice Coltrane's "Something About John Coltrane." My poem uses a durational form, one that is the length of Coltrane's recorded album version of the song.

The poem also takes as its source material the sonic landscape and material of Marion Brown's "Afternoon of a Georgia Faun," Aretha Franklin's live album *Amazing Grace*, and Mahalia Jackson's singing of "Just a Closer Walk with Thee" at the Newport Jazz Festival in 1970.

"The tiny rack a seed makes cracking open in the dark" is quoted from Ross Gay's "Weeping" in *Catalog of Unabashed Gratitude*.

"No longer shall you take things second or third hand" is from Walt Whitman's "Song of Myself."

"ODE TO PABLO NERUDA'S 'ODE TO A LEMON'"

"Out of lemon flowers loosed on the moonlight," "barbarous gold," and "breast and nipple" come from Pablo Neruda's "Ode to a Lemon," http://www.phys.unm.edu/~tw/fas/yits/archive/neruda_odetoalemon.html.

"Scipio baptized 1760 likely Negro boy / About a month old to be given away" comes from Eric Slauter's article, "Looking for Scipio Moorhead," on Scipio Moorhead, an enslaved man and artist who made the famous engraving of Phillis Wheatley for the frontispiece of Phillis Wheatley's first book of poems, *Poems on Various Subjects, Religious and Moral*, the first book of poems published by an enslaved African in the United States. Wheatley also published a poem in *Poems on Various Subjects, Religious and Moral* dedicated to Scipio.

"The way we lay we mimed a body of water" is from Nathaniel Mackey's "Eye on the Scarecrow."

"Everywhere the bucks went clattering / The police bristled in the way" is a pejoration, a corruption of Wallace Stevens's "Every time the bucks went clattering /. . . A firecat bristled in the way" from "Earthy Anecdotes." Stevens is saying something about poetic form as am I—and race, too—you dig?

"Me and you / Your momma and your cousin too / Rolling down the strip on Vogues / Waking up slamming Cadillac doors" is from Outkast's "Elevators (Me and You)." Lyrics © BMG Rights Management.

"DRAPETOMANIA, OR JAMES BALDWIN AS AN IMPROVISATION"

"Drapetomania" was the alleged mental condition that enslaved folks were said to have when they ran away from their plantations and masters, seeking freedom.

"Battlefield where the moon says I love you" is from the title of an epic poem by Frank Stanford.

Notes on the State of Virginia is a book by Thomas Jefferson wherein he writes: "Religion indeed has produced a Phyllis Whately [sic]; but it could not produce a poet. The compositions published under her name are below the dignity of criticism." I obviously disagree with Jefferson, but this sort of criticism is the beginning of the American (literary) critical tradition that cannot comprehend the largesse of Black aesthetic productions or Black life. This perception of a lack of erudition or aesthetic rigor is obviously solely a product of white supremacy and the intellectual shortcomings of the critic (i.e., Jefferson). Toni Morrison takes on this lack of imagination, this lack of vision, in *Playing in the Dark: Whiteness and the Literary Imagination*. My poem seeks to abjectly play in the poetics of profligacy, of fugitivity—the fugitivity of running away from your captor.

"ESPÍRITU SANTO TAMBIÉN . . ."

This poem is inspired by a field recording done by the anthropologist and musician Alex Chávez.

"The naked human body is the grave in blossom" is from Larry Levis's "Sleeping Lioness."

"FRAGMENT 107"

"Do I long for my virginity" is a riff off a fragment of Sappho translated by Anne Carson in *If Not, Winter: Fragments of Sappho*.

"AMERICAN RUNNER"

"O song of the river blood, o blood of the river song" is a riff off Jericho Brown's "Langston Blue" and Terrance Hayes's "A Small Novel."

"LEAF-SIGH AND BRAY"

The quote "ecstasy is more leaf-sigh than bray" comes from Toni Morrison's novel *Jazz*.

"CAUGHT IN A BLACK DOORWAY"

"Touching the stubble of a priest's face / Caught in a black doorway of a church / As he was coming out into the cold winter street" is from David Ferry's "Reading Arthur Gold's Poem 'Rome, December 1973.'"

"FUTURE, FROM BEYOND THE VOICE OF GOD"

When boxer Jack Johnson was asked by a reporter why White women love Black men (because Johnson was known to date White women during a time in the United States when interracial dating was not only taboo, but illegal), Johnson replied: "Because we eat cold eels and think distant thoughts," which I believe is one of the best answers to a question that should not have been asked. It is now my default answer to any question that doesn't make a lick of sense.

"BY BEAUTY, FROM BEYOND THE VOICE OF GOD"

The quoted section in the second half of the poem is from the biography of Sun Ra, *Space is the Place: The Lives and Times of Sun Ra* by John Szwed. The quote is from an interview wherein Sun Ra illustrates the difference between God and the Creator.

"I CAN DRINK THE DISTANCE, OR FIRE IN THE LAKE"

"As a stone in love" is quoted from "Orpheus" in *Songs of Mihyar the Damascene* by Adonis (translated by Kareem James Abu-Zeid and Ivan Eubanks).

"I wound the water's face" is quoted from "Land of Enchantment" in *Songs of Mihyar the Damascene.*

"JOURNEY TO SATCHIDANANDA"

The title of the poem comes from Alice Coltrane's song, which is also the title of her album.

"How the Stars Understand Us" and "Fire Gotten Brighter" are the titles of poems by Christopher Gilbert from his first book of poems, *Across the Mutual Landscape.*

"Knowing nothing lives as foreignness" is from "Kodak and Chris Walk the Mutual Landscape" in *Across the Mutual Landscape.*